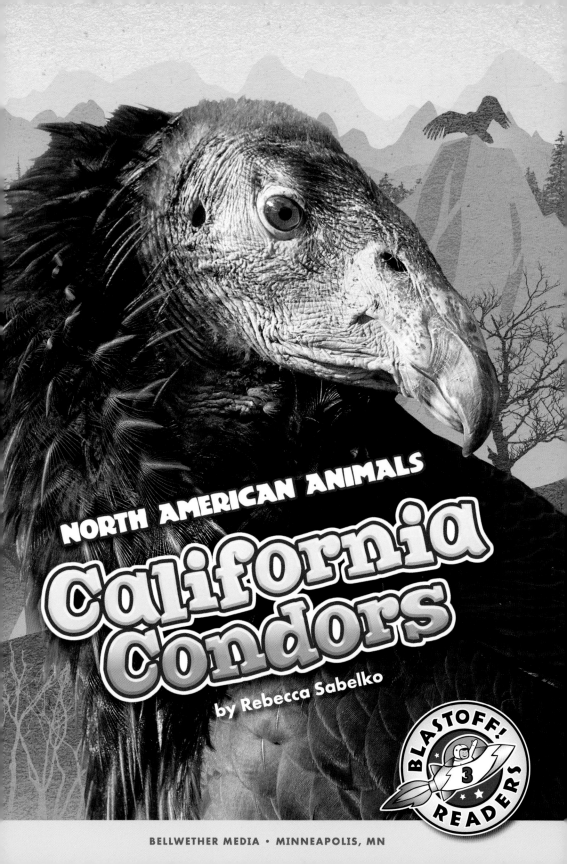

NORTH AMERICAN ANIMALS

California Condors

by Rebecca Sabelko

BELLWETHER MEDIA • MINNEAPOLIS, MN

Note to Librarians, Teachers, and Parents:

Blastoff! Readers are carefully developed by literacy experts and combine standards-based content with developmentally appropriate text.

Level 1 provides the most support through repetition of high-frequency words, light text, predictable sentence patterns, and strong visual support.

Level 2 offers early readers a bit more challenge through varied simple sentences, increased text load, and less repetition of high-frequency words.

Level 3 advances early-fluent readers toward fluency through increased text and concept load, less reliance on visuals, longer sentences, and more literary language.

Level 4 builds reading stamina by providing more text per page, increased use of punctuation, greater variation in sentence patterns, and increasingly challenging vocabulary.

Level 5 encourages children to move from "learning to read" to "reading to learn" by providing even more text, varied writing styles, and less familiar topics.

Whichever book is right for your reader, Blastoff! Readers are the perfect books to build confidence and encourage a love of reading that will last a lifetime!

This edition first published in 2019 by Bellwether Media, Inc.

No part of this publication may be reproduced in whole or in part without written permission of the publisher. For information regarding permission, write to Bellwether Media, Inc., Attention: Permissions Department, 6012 Blue Circle Drive, Minnetonka, MN 55343.

Library of Congress Cataloging-in-Publication Data

Names: Sabelko, Rebecca, author.
Title: California Condors / by Rebecca Sabelko.
Description: Minneapolis, MN : Bellwether Media, Inc., 2019. | Series:
    Blastoff! Readers. North American Animals | Audience: Age 5-8. | Audience:
    Grade K to 3. | Includes bibliographical references and index.
Identifiers: LCCN 2017056260 (print) | LCCN 2018004965 (ebook) | ISBN
    9781626177963 (hardcover : alk. paper) | ISBN 9781681035215 (ebook)
Subjects: LCSH: California condor–North America–Juvenile literature.
Classification: LCC QL696.C53 (ebook) | LCC QL696.C53 S23 2019 (print) | DDC
    598.9/2–dc23
LC record available at https://lccn.loc.gov/2017056260

Editor: Betsy Rathburn   Designer: Josh Brink

Printed in the United States of America, North Mankato, MN.

Table of **Contents**

What Are California Condors? 4

Soaring Giants   8

Skydiving Scavengers   14

Nest Life   18

Glossary   22

To Learn More   23

Index   24

What Are California Condors?

California condors are North America's largest flying birds. They are sometimes mistaken for small planes!

In the Wild

N
W
E
S

California condor range = ▢

conservation status: critically endangered

Extinct

Extinct in the Wild

Critically Endangered

Endangered

Vulnerable

Near Threatened

Least Concern

These birds are found in parts of Mexico and the southwestern United States. They soar in wide-open skies searching for **carrion**.

These **raptors** once flew across the west coast of North America. But they almost went **extinct**.

Today, about 300 California condors live in their natural **habitat**. They **perch** on high cliffs and trees in rocky forests.

Soaring Giants

California condors have long, wide wings. They reach up to 10 feet (3 meters) across!

This giant **wingspan** helps condors soar for hours at a time. They can cover hundreds of miles in one flight!

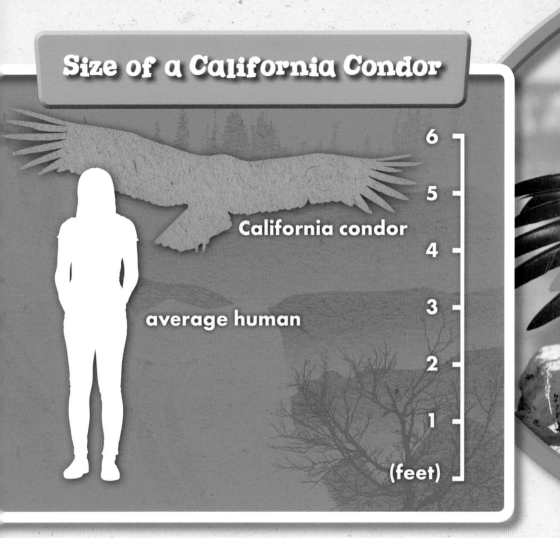

Size of a California Condor

California condor

average human

6
5
4
3
2
1
(feet)

These heavy birds can weigh up to 22 pounds (10 kilograms)! Their size makes it hard to take flight.

Jumping from tall trees or cliffs helps California condors get into the air.

Black feathers cover condor
bodies. They have white
markings under each wing.

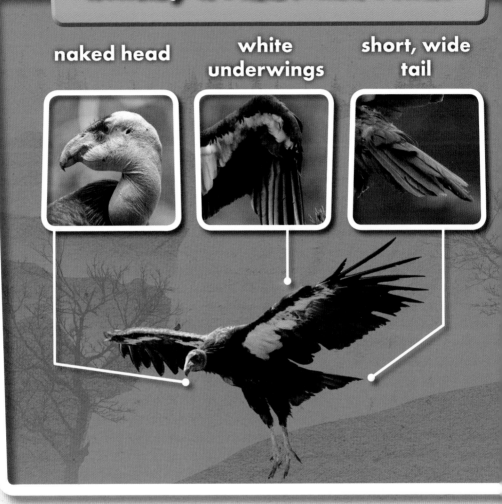

Identify a California Condor

naked head

white underwings

short, wide tail

Adult California condors have hairless heads and necks. Their skin is a bright yellow-orange color.

Skydiving Scavengers

California condors use their excellent eyesight to find food. They **scavenge** for **carcasses** killed by other animals.

These **carnivores** dive from the sky when they spot food. Sharp beaks rip the meat apart. Condors even swallow bone chips!

crop

California condors take their food to go. They store up to 3 pounds (1.4 kilograms) of food. They keep it in throat pouches called **crops**.

They can live up to two weeks between meals!

Male and female California condors nest together on high cliffs. Then, females lay one egg. The egg **hatches** in a couple of months. Out comes a fluffy white **chick**!

Baby Facts

Name for babies: chicks

Number of eggs laid: 1 egg

Time spent inside egg: about 2 months

Time spent with parents: about 1 year

Soon, the **nestling** begins to play. It stays close to the nest.

The **fledgling** begins exploring the sky with mom and dad. Soar high, young condor!

Glossary

carcasses—the dead bodies of animals

carnivores—animals that only eat meat

carrion—the rotting meat of a dead animal

chick—a baby California condor

crops—pouches in the throats of many birds where food is stored

extinct—no longer existing

fledgling—young birds that have feathers for flight

habitat—land with certain types of plants, animals, and weather

hatches—breaks out of an egg

nestling—a chick that cannot fly yet

perch—to sit in a high spot

raptors—large birds that search for animals for food; raptors have excellent eyesight and powerful talons.

scavenge—to feed on carrion

wingspan—the distance between the tip of one wing to the tip of the other

To Learn More

AT THE LIBRARY

Lanser, Amanda. *California Condor*. Minneapolis, Minn.: ABDO Publishing, 2017.

Leighton, Christina. *Golden Eagles*. Minneapolis, Minn.: Bellwether Media, 2017.

Waxman, Laura Hamilton. *California Condor: Wide-winged Soaring Birds*. Minneapolis, Minn.: Learner Publications, 2016.

ON THE WEB

Learning more about California condors is as easy as 1, 2, 3.

1. Go to www.factsurfer.com.

2. Enter "California condors" into the search box.

3. Click the "Surf" button and you will see a list of related web sites.

With factsurfer.com, finding more information is just a click away.

Index

beaks, 15
bodies, 12
carcasses, 14
carnivores, 15
carrion, 5
chick, 18, 19
cliffs, 7, 11, 18
crops, 16
egg, 18, 19
extinct, 6
eyesight, 14
feathers, 12
females, 18
fledgling, 21
fly, 4, 6, 9, 10, 21
food, 5, 14, 15, 16, 17
forests, 7
habitat, 7
heads, 13
males, 18
Mexico, 5
necks, 13
nest, 18, 20
nestling, 20

perch, 7
range, 5, 6
raptors, 6
scavenge, 14
size, 4, 8, 10
skin, 13
status, 5
trees, 7, 11
underwings, 12, 13
United States, 5
wings, 8, 9, 12, 13
wingspan, 8, 9